Spotter's Guide

WILD FLOWERS

Christopher Humphries
Botany Department of the British Museum (Natural History)

Illustrated by Hilary Burn

with additional illustrations by Joyce Bee
and Christine Howes

USBORNE

Contents

Designed by
Sally Burrough

Edited by
Jessica Datta and
Sue Jacquemier

Printed by
Mateu Cromo Artes Graficas, S.A.
Madrid, Spain.

First published in 1978 by Usborne Publishing
Limited, 20 Garrick Street, London WC2

Second impression 1978

Reprinted 1979

Text and Artwork © 1978 by
Usborne Publishing Limited

How to Use this Book

This book is an identification guide to some of the wild flowers of Britain and Europe. Take it with you when you go out spotting. The flowers are arranged by colour to make it easy for you to look them up.

The pictures in circles next to the main illustrations show close-ups of flowers or sometimes the fruits or seeds of the plant. These will help you to identify the flowers at different times of year.

For example, this Rosebay Willowherb appears in the section of the book that shows pink flowers. The picture in the circle below shows a close-up of a seed from this plant.

Seed of Rosebay Willowherb (seeds can be seen after the plant has finished flowering)

Top of plant

The height is given in centimetres (cm)

Rosebay Willowherb

Ground Level

The description next to each flower will also help you to identify it. The plants are not drawn to scale but the description gives you their average height measured from the ground. The last line of the description tells you the months when you usually see each plant in flower.

Beside the description is a small blank circle. Each time you spot a flower, make a tick like this in the correct circle.

Areas Covered by this Book

The green area on this map shows the countries covered by this book. Not all the flowers that grow in these areas appear in the book. Some of the flowers shown are very rare in Britain, or do not grow here at all, but are common in other countries of Europe. Try to spot them if you go on holiday abroad.

Scorecard

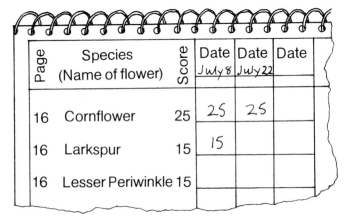

Page	Species (Name of flower)	Score	Date July 8	Date July 22	Date
16	Cornflower	25	25	25	
16	Larkspur	15	15		
16	Lesser Periwinkle	15			

The scorecard at the end of the book gives you a score for each flower you spot. A common flower scores 5 points, and a very rare one is worth 25 points. If you like, you can add up your score after a day out spotting. As some of the flowers are very difficult to find in the wild, you can tick off rare flowers if you see them on television or in a film.

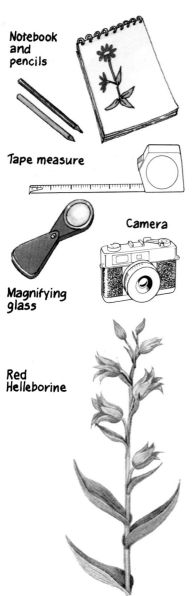

Notebook and pencils

Tape measure

Magnifying glass

Camera

Red Helleborine

What to Take

When you go out to spot flowers, take this book, a notebook and pencils with you so that you can record your finds. Take a tape measure to measure the height of plants and the length of runners. A magnifying glass will help you to take a closer look at the parts of flower heads. It is also useful for examining insects you may see on plants. Take a camera, if you have one, to photograph flowers (see page 58). Remember to make notes about the flowers you photograph.

Draw flowers you spot and note down details about them. Be sure to include the height of the plant, the colour and shape of the flower head and the leaves, and the place where the plant grows. If you find a flower that is not in this book, your drawing will help you to identify it from other books later. There is a list of useful books on page 59.

Protecting Wild Flowers

Be careful not to tread on young plants or to break their stems.

Many wild plants that were once common are now rare, because people have picked and dug up so many. It is against the law to dig up any wild plant by the roots, or to pick certain rare plants such as the Red Helleborine. If you pick wild flowers, they will die. Leave them for others to enjoy. It is much better to draw or photograph flowers, so that you and other people can see them again.

If you think you have found a rare plant, let your local nature conservation club know about it as soon as you can, so they can help protect it. You can get their address from your local library or Town Hall.

These pictures show the different parts of plants, and explain some of the words that appear in the book. When you are examining a plant, look closely at the flower head and the leaves. These will help you to identify it.

Flowers

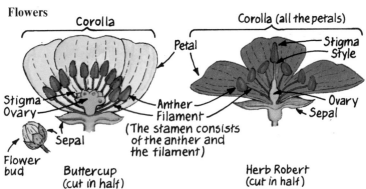

Corolla

Petal

Stigma
Style

Stigma
Ovary

Anther
Filament
(The stamen consists of the anther and the filament)

Ovary
Sepal

Sepal

Flower bud

Buttercup
(cut in half)

Corolla (all the petals)

Herb Robert
(cut in half)

The stigma, style and ovary are the female parts of the flower, and the stamens are the male parts. Pollen from the stamens is received by the stigma. It causes seeds to grow inside the ovary.

The petals of some flowers are joined together.

Corolla {

Lily of the Valley

The petals of some flowers form a tube called a spur.

Spur

Petal

Larkspur

Fruits and Seeds

The seeds of a plant are usually surrounded by the fruit. Fruits of different plants are of different sizes and shapes. They usually appear after the petals have withered and fallen off. Here are two examples.

Seed

Blackberry fruit
(the seeds are inside)

Shepherd's Purse fruit
(cut in half)

Leaves

There are many different leaf shapes, and leaves can also be arranged in different ways on the stem.

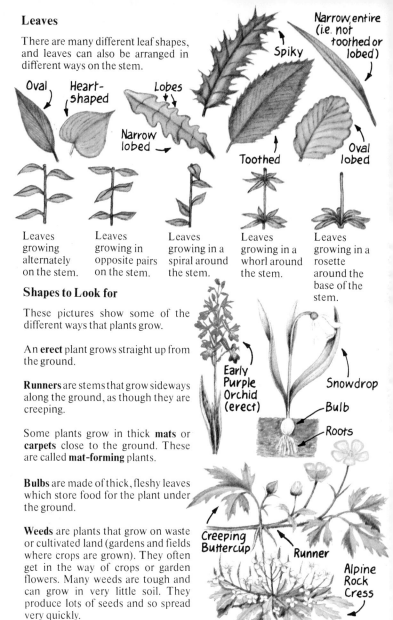

Spiky

Narrow, entire (i.e. not toothed or lobed)

Oval

Heart-shaped

Lobes

Narrow lobed

Toothed

Oval lobed

Leaves growing alternately on the stem.

Leaves growing in opposite pairs on the stem.

Leaves growing in a spiral around the stem.

Leaves growing in a whorl around the stem.

Leaves growing in a rosette around the base of the stem.

Shapes to Look for

These pictures show some of the different ways that plants grow.

An **erect** plant grows straight up from the ground.

Runners are stems that grow sideways along the ground, as though they are creeping.

Some plants grow in thick **mats** or **carpets** close to the ground. These are called **mat-forming** plants.

Bulbs are made of thick, fleshy leaves which store food for the plant under the ground.

Weeds are plants that grow on waste or cultivated land (gardens and fields where crops are grown). They often get in the way of crops or garden flowers. Many weeds are tough and can grow in very little soil. They produce lots of seeds and so spread very quickly.

Early Purple Orchid (erect)

Snowdrop

Bulb

Roots

Creeping Buttercup

Runner

Alpine Rock Cress

(mat-forming)

7

Look for these flowers in damp places, such as ditches, marshes and water meadows.

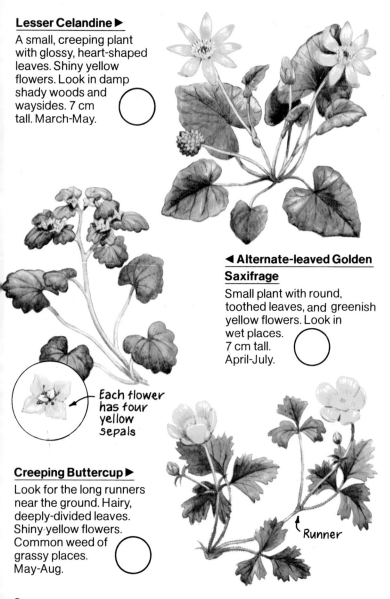

Lesser Celandine ▶

A small, creeping plant with glossy, heart-shaped leaves. Shiny yellow flowers. Look in damp shady woods and waysides. 7 cm tall. March-May.

◀ Alternate-leaved Golden Saxifrage

Small plant with round, toothed leaves, and greenish yellow flowers. Look in wet places. 7 cm tall. April-July.

Each flower has four yellow sepals

Creeping Buttercup ▶

Look for the long runners near the ground. Hairy, deeply-divided leaves. Shiny yellow flowers. Common weed of grassy places. May-Aug.

Runner

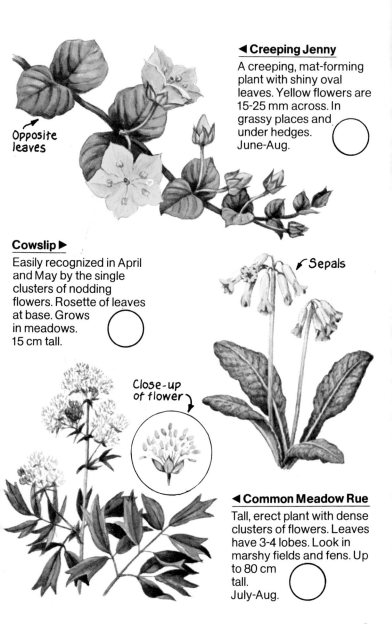

◄ Creeping Jenny

A creeping, mat-forming plant with shiny oval leaves. Yellow flowers are 15-25 mm across. In grassy places and under hedges. June-Aug.

Opposite leaves

Cowslip ►

Easily recognized in April and May by the single clusters of nodding flowers. Rosette of leaves at base. Grows in meadows. 15 cm tall.

Sepals

Close-up of flower

◄ Common Meadow Rue

Tall, erect plant with dense clusters of flowers. Leaves have 3-4 lobes. Look in marshy fields and fens. Up to 80 cm tall. July-Aug.

Look for these flowers, and those on page 11, in woods, hedgerows and heaths.

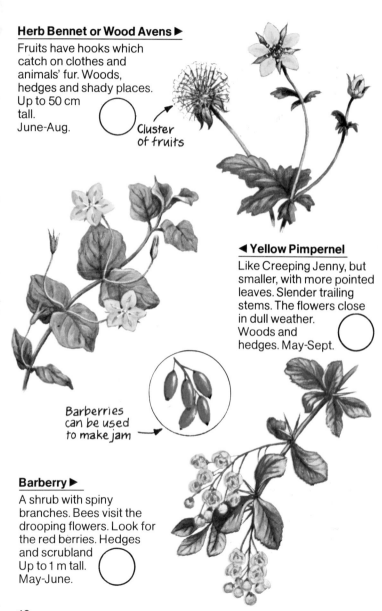

Herb Bennet or Wood Avens ▶

Fruits have hooks which catch on clothes and animals' fur. Woods, hedges and shady places. Up to 50 cm tall. June-Aug.

Cluster of fruits

◀ Yellow Pimpernel

Like Creeping Jenny, but smaller, with more pointed leaves. Slender trailing stems. The flowers close in dull weather. Woods and hedges. May-Sept.

Barberries can be used to make jam →

Barberry ▶

A shrub with spiny branches. Bees visit the drooping flowers. Look for the red berries. Hedges and scrubland Up to 1 m tall. May-June.

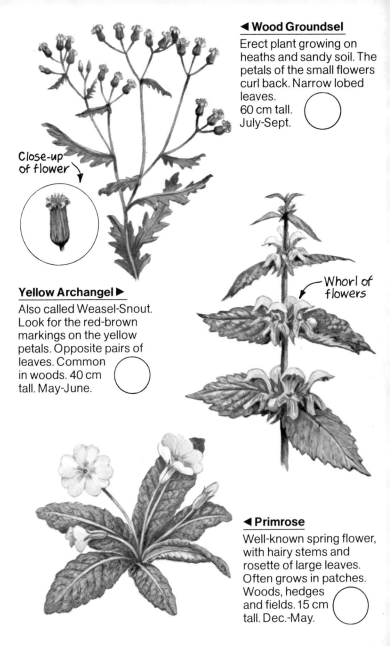

◀ Wood Groundsel

Erect plant growing on heaths and sandy soil. The petals of the small flowers curl back. Narrow lobed leaves.
60 cm tall.
July-Sept.

Close-up of flower ↘

Yellow Archangel ▶

Also called Weasel-Snout. Look for the red-brown markings on the yellow petals. Opposite pairs of leaves. Common in woods. 40 cm tall. May-June.

Whorl of flowers

◀ Primrose

Well-known spring flower, with hairy stems and rosette of large leaves. Often grows in patches. Woods, hedges and fields. 15 cm tall. Dec.-May.

Look for these flowers, and those on page 13, in open grassy places, such as heaths and commons.

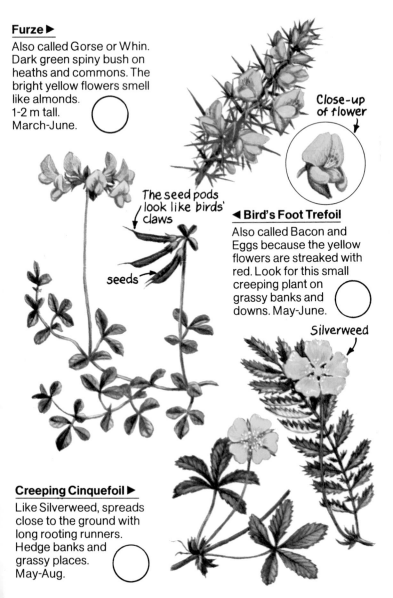

Furze ▶

Also called Gorse or Whin. Dark green spiny bush on heaths and commons. The bright yellow flowers smell like almonds.
1-2 m tall.
March-June.

Close-up of flower

The seed pods look like birds' claws

seeds

◀ Bird's Foot Trefoil

Also called Bacon and Eggs because the yellow flowers are streaked with red. Look for this small creeping plant on grassy banks and downs. May-June.

Silverweed

Creeping Cinquefoil ▶

Like Silverweed, spreads close to the ground with long rooting runners. Hedge banks and grassy places.
May-Aug.

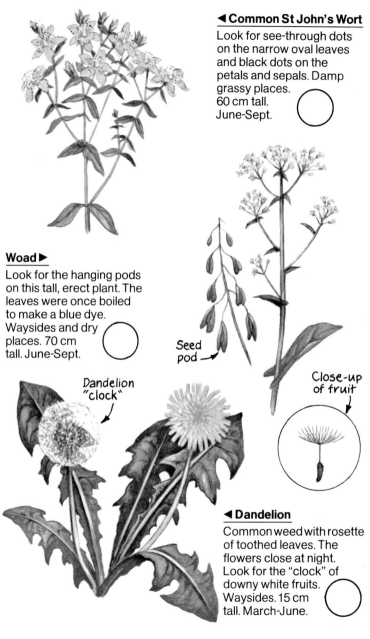

◀ Common St John's Wort

Look for see-through dots on the narrow oval leaves and black dots on the petals and sepals. Damp grassy places.
60 cm tall.
June-Sept.

Woad ▶

Look for the hanging pods on this tall, erect plant. The leaves were once boiled to make a blue dye. Waysides and dry places. 70 cm tall. June-Sept.

Seed pod

Dandelion "clock"

Close-up of fruit

◀ Dandelion

Common weed with rosette of toothed leaves. The flowers close at night. Look for the "clock" of downy white fruits. Waysides. 15 cm tall. March-June.

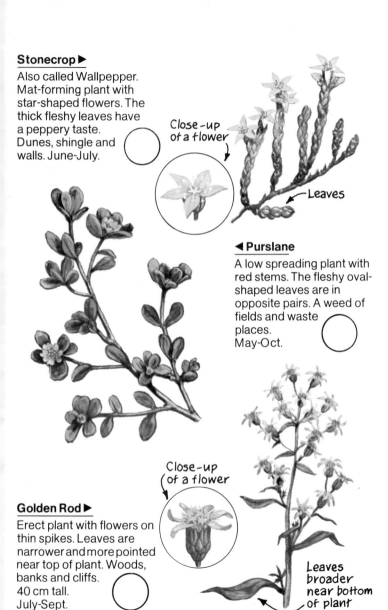

Stonecrop ▶

Also called Wallpepper.
Mat-forming plant with
star-shaped flowers. The
thick fleshy leaves have
a peppery taste.
Dunes, shingle and
walls. June-July.

Close-up
of a flower

Leaves

◀ Purslane

A low spreading plant with
red stems. The fleshy oval-
shaped leaves are in
opposite pairs. A weed of
fields and waste
places.
May-Oct.

Close-up
of a flower

Golden Rod ▶

Erect plant with flowers on
thin spikes. Leaves are
narrower and more pointed
near top of plant. Woods,
banks and cliffs.
40 cm tall.
July-Sept.

Leaves
broader
near bottom
of plant

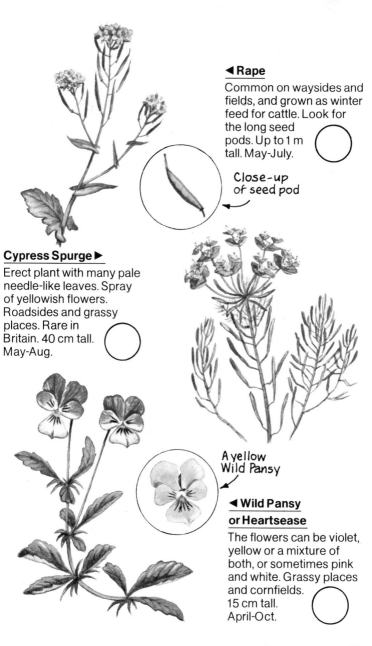

◀ Rape

Common on waysides and fields, and grown as winter feed for cattle. Look for the long seed pods. Up to 1 m tall. May-July.

Close-up of seed pod

Cypress Spurge ▶

Erect plant with many pale needle-like leaves. Spray of yellowish flowers. Roadsides and grassy places. Rare in Britain. 40 cm tall. May-Aug.

A yellow Wild Pansy

◀ Wild Pansy or Heartsease

The flowers can be violet, yellow or a mixture of both, or sometimes pink and white. Grassy places and cornfields. 15 cm tall. April-Oct.

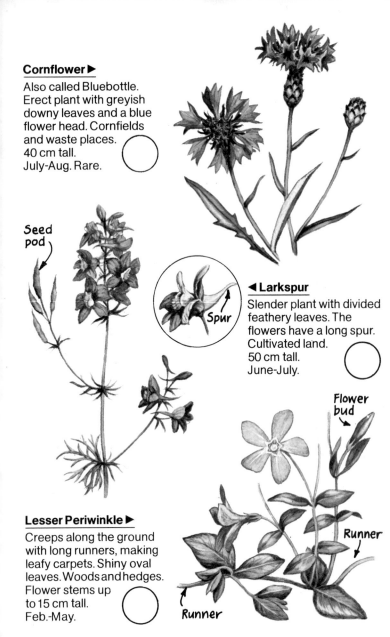

Cornflower ▶

Also called Bluebottle.
Erect plant with greyish
downy leaves and a blue
flower head. Cornfields
and waste places.
40 cm tall.
July-Aug. Rare.

Seed
pod

◀ Larkspur

Slender plant with divided
feathery leaves. The
flowers have a long spur.
Cultivated land.
50 cm tall.
June-July.

Spur

Flower
bud

Lesser Periwinkle ▶

Creeps along the ground
with long runners, making
leafy carpets. Shiny oval
leaves. Woods and hedges.
Flower stems up
to 15 cm tall.
Feb.-May.

Runner

Runner

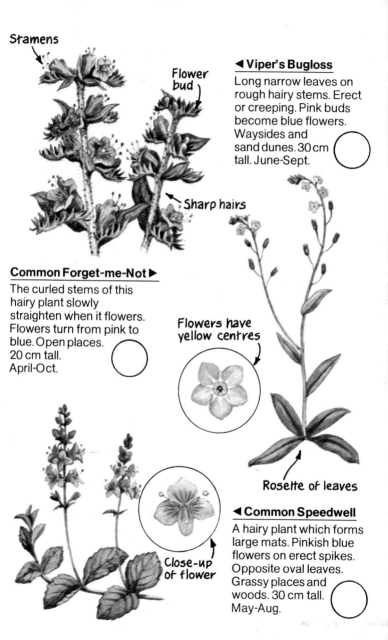

Stamens

Flower bud

Sharp hairs

◄ Viper's Bugloss
Long narrow leaves on rough hairy stems. Erect or creeping. Pink buds become blue flowers. Waysides and sand dunes. 30 cm tall. June-Sept.

Common Forget-me-Not ►
The curled stems of this hairy plant slowly straighten when it flowers. Flowers turn from pink to blue. Open places. 20 cm tall. April-Oct.

Flowers have yellow centres

Rosette of leaves

Close-up of flower

◄ Common Speedwell
A hairy plant which forms large mats. Pinkish blue flowers on erect spikes. Opposite oval leaves. Grassy places and woods. 30 cm tall. May-Aug.

Look for the flowers shown on this page in damp places.

Common Monkshood ▶

Also called Wolfsbane.
Notice hood on flowers
and the deeply-divided
leaves. Near streams and
in damp woods.
70 cm tall.
June-Sept.

*Flower is
shaped like a
monk's hood*

◀ Brooklime

Creeping plant with erect
reddish stems. Shiny oval
leaves in opposite pairs.
Used to be eaten in
salads. Wet
places. 30 cm tall.
May-Sept.

Bugle ▶

Creeping plant with erect
flower spikes. Purplish
stem is hairy on two
sides. Forms carpets in
damp woods.
10-20 cm tall.
May-June.

*Close-up of
bugle-shaped
flower*

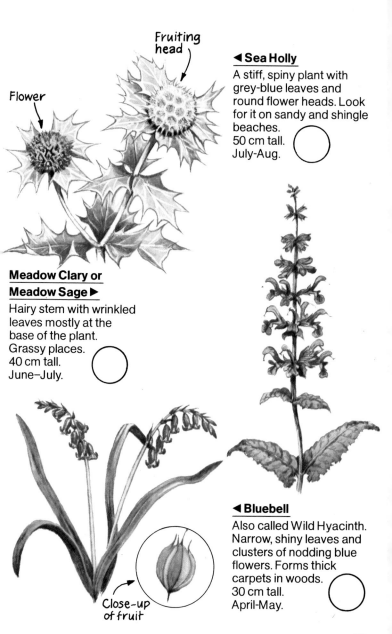

Fruiting head

Flower

◀ Sea Holly
A stiff, spiny plant with grey-blue leaves and round flower heads. Look for it on sandy and shingle beaches.
50 cm tall.
July-Aug.

Meadow Clary or Meadow Sage ▶
Hairy stem with wrinkled leaves mostly at the base of the plant. Grassy places.
40 cm tall.
June–July.

◀ Bluebell
Also called Wild Hyacinth. Narrow, shiny leaves and clusters of nodding blue flowers. Forms thick carpets in woods.
30 cm tall.
April-May.

Close-up of fruit

Look for the flowers shown on this page in woods or hedges.

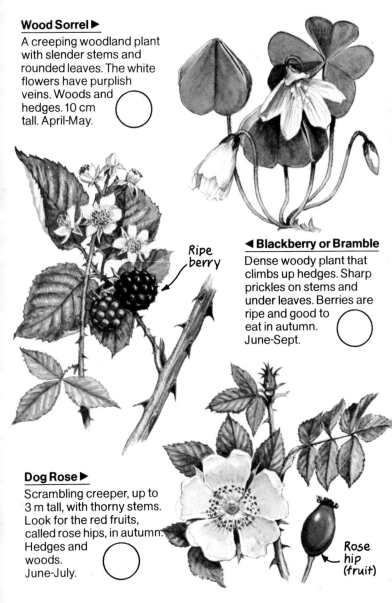

Wood Sorrel ▶

A creeping woodland plant with slender stems and rounded leaves. The white flowers have purplish veins. Woods and hedges. 10 cm tall. April-May.

Ripe berry

◀ Blackberry or Bramble

Dense woody plant that climbs up hedges. Sharp prickles on stems and under leaves. Berries are ripe and good to eat in autumn. June-Sept.

Dog Rose ▶

Scrambling creeper, up to 3 m tall, with thorny stems. Look for the red fruits, called rose hips, in autumn. Hedges and woods. June-July.

Rose hip (fruit)

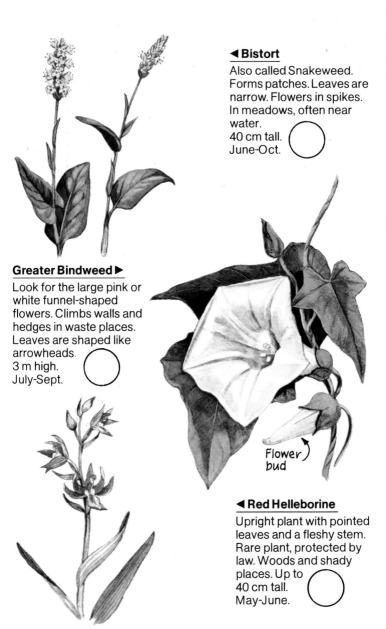

◀ Bistort

Also called Snakeweed. Forms patches. Leaves are narrow. Flowers in spikes. In meadows, often near water.
40 cm tall.
June-Oct.

Greater Bindweed ▶

Look for the large pink or white funnel-shaped flowers. Climbs walls and hedges in waste places. Leaves are shaped like arrowheads.
3 m high.
July-Sept.

Flower bud

◀ Red Helleborine

Upright plant with pointed leaves and a fleshy stem. Rare plant, protected by law. Woods and shady places. Up to 40 cm tall.
May-June.

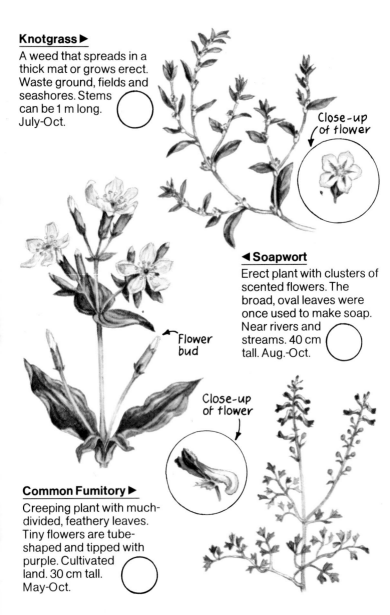

Knotgrass ▶

A weed that spreads in a thick mat or grows erect. Waste ground, fields and seashores. Stems can be 1 m long. July-Oct.

Close-up of flower

◀ Soapwort

Erect plant with clusters of scented flowers. The broad, oval leaves were once used to make soap. Near rivers and streams. 40 cm tall. Aug.-Oct.

Flower bud

Close-up of flower

Common Fumitory ▶

Creeping plant with much-divided, feathery leaves. Tiny flowers are tube-shaped and tipped with purple. Cultivated land. 30 cm tall. May-Oct.

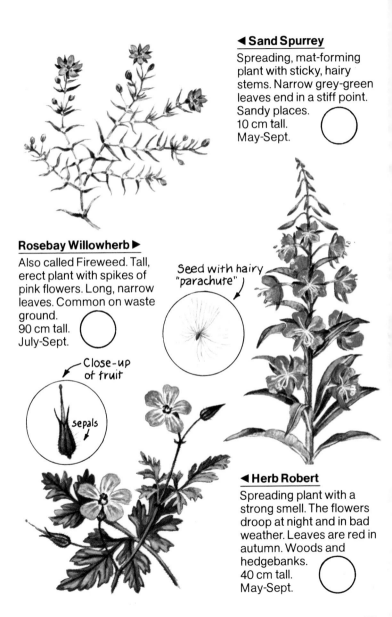

◄ Sand Spurrey

Spreading, mat-forming plant with sticky, hairy stems. Narrow grey-green leaves end in a stiff point. Sandy places.
10 cm tall.
May-Sept.

Rosebay Willowherb ►

Also called Fireweed. Tall, erect plant with spikes of pink flowers. Long, narrow leaves. Common on waste ground.
90 cm tall.
July-Sept.

Seed with hairy "parachute"

Close-up of fruit

sepals

◄ Herb Robert

Spreading plant with a strong smell. The flowers droop at night and in bad weather. Leaves are red in autumn. Woods and hedgebanks.
40 cm tall.
May-Sept.

Look for these flowers on heaths and moors.

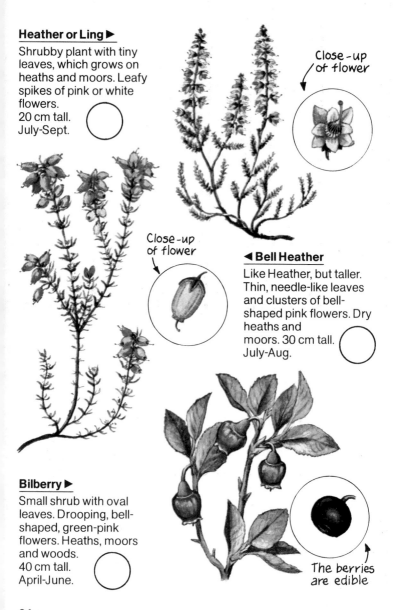

Heather or Ling ▶

Shrubby plant with tiny leaves, which grows on heaths and moors. Leafy spikes of pink or white flowers.
20 cm tall.
July-Sept.

Close-up of flower

Close-up of flower

◀ Bell Heather

Like Heather, but taller. Thin, needle-like leaves and clusters of bell-shaped pink flowers. Dry heaths and moors. 30 cm tall. July-Aug.

Bilberry ▶

Small shrub with oval leaves. Drooping, bell-shaped, green-pink flowers. Heaths, moors and woods.
40 cm tall.
April-June.

The berries are edible

Look for these flowers in dry, grassy places.

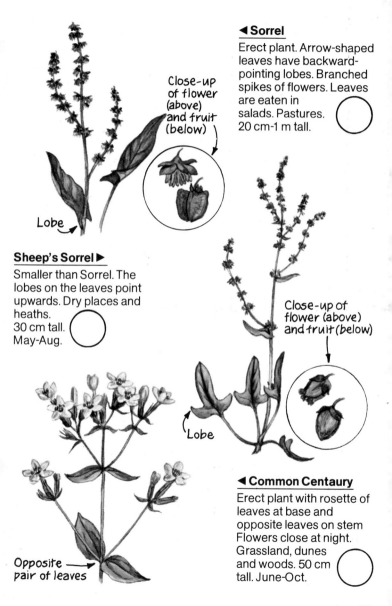

Close-up
of flower
(above)
and fruit
(below)

◄ Sorrel
Erect plant. Arrow-shaped
leaves have backward-
pointing lobes. Branched
spikes of flowers. Leaves
are eaten in
salads. Pastures.
20 cm-1 m tall.

Lobe

Sheep's Sorrel ►
Smaller than Sorrel. The
lobes on the leaves point
upwards. Dry places and
heaths.
30 cm tall.
May-Aug.

Close-up of
flower (above)
and fruit (below)

Lobe

◄ Common Centaury
Erect plant with rosette of
leaves at base and
opposite leaves on stem
Flowers close at night.
Grassland, dunes
and woods. 50 cm
tall. June-Oct.

Opposite
pair of leaves

Ragged Robin ▶

Flowers have ragged pink petals. Erect plant with a forked stem and narrow, pointed leaves. Damp meadows, marshes and woods.
30-70 cm tall.
May-June.

A bract is a kind of small leaf near the flower

Grooved stem

◀ Knapweed or Hard-head

Erect plant with brush-like pink flowers growing from black bracts. Grassland and waysides.
40 cm tall.
June-Sept.

Hemp Agrimony ▶

Tough, erect plant with downy stem. Grows in patches in damp places. Attracts butterflies.
Up to 120 cm tall.
July–Sept.

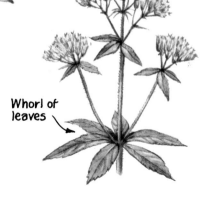

Whorl of leaves

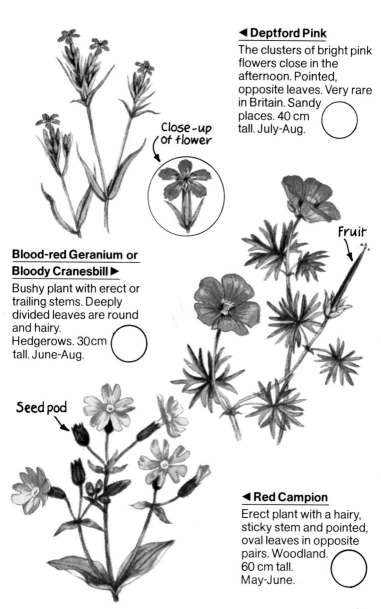

◄ Deptford Pink

The clusters of bright pink flowers close in the afternoon. Pointed, opposite leaves. Very rare in Britain. Sandy places. 40 cm tall. July-Aug.

Close-up of flower

Fruit

Blood-red Geranium or Bloody Cranesbill ►

Bushy plant with erect or trailing stems. Deeply divided leaves are round and hairy. Hedgerows. 30cm tall. June-Aug.

Seed pod

◄ Red Campion

Erect plant with a hairy, sticky stem and pointed, oval leaves in opposite pairs. Woodland. 60 cm tall. May-June.

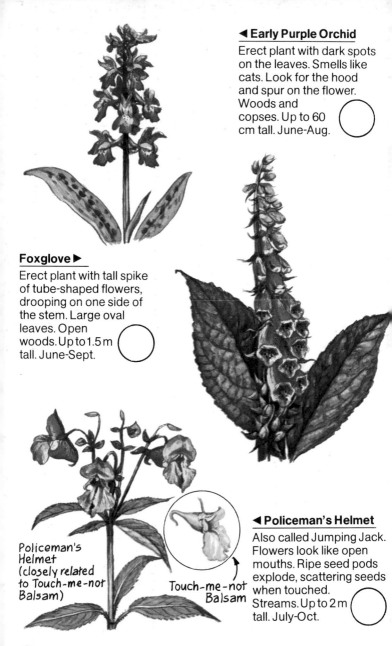

◄ Early Purple Orchid
Erect plant with dark spots on the leaves. Smells like cats. Look for the hood and spur on the flower. Woods and copses. Up to 60 cm tall. June-Aug.

Foxglove ►
Erect plant with tall spike of tube-shaped flowers, drooping on one side of the stem. Large oval leaves. Open woods. Up to 1.5 m tall. June-Sept.

Policeman's Helmet (closely related to Touch-me-not Balsam)

Touch-me-not Balsam

◄ Policeman's Helmet
Also called Jumping Jack. Flowers look like open mouths. Ripe seed pods explode, scattering seeds when touched. Streams. Up to 2 m tall. July-Oct.

Look for the flowers shown on this page in woods or hedgerows.

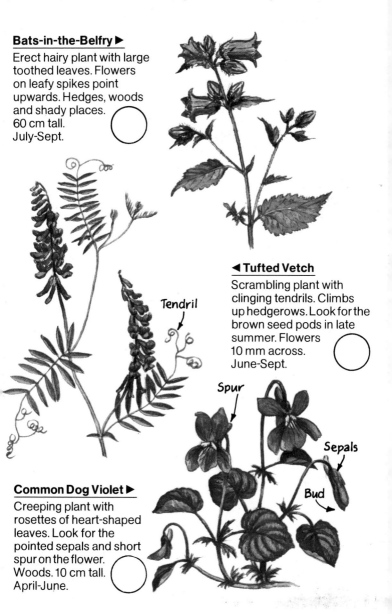

Bats-in-the-Belfry ▶
Erect hairy plant with large toothed leaves. Flowers on leafy spikes point upwards. Hedges, woods and shady places. 60 cm tall. July-Sept.

Tendril

◀ Tufted Vetch
Scrambling plant with clinging tendrils. Climbs up hedgerows. Look for the brown seed pods in late summer. Flowers 10 mm across. June-Sept.

Spur

Sepals

Bud

Common Dog Violet ▶
Creeping plant with rosettes of heart-shaped leaves. Look for the pointed sepals and short spur on the flower. Woods. 10 cm tall. April-June.

Look in fields and other grassy places for these flowers.

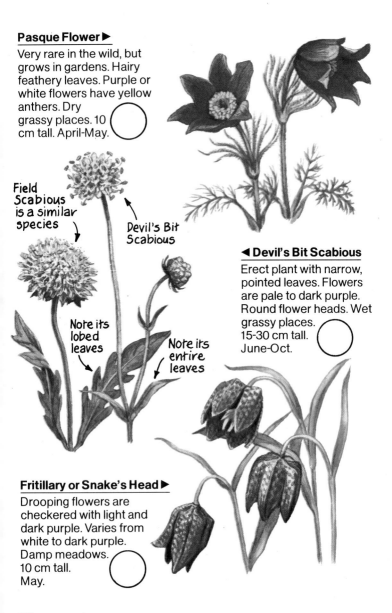

Pasque Flower ▶

Very rare in the wild, but grows in gardens. Hairy feathery leaves. Purple or white flowers have yellow anthers. Dry grassy places. 10 cm tall. April-May.

Field Scabious is a similar species

Devil's Bit Scabious

Note its lobed leaves

Note its entire leaves

◀ Devil's Bit Scabious

Erect plant with narrow, pointed leaves. Flowers are pale to dark purple. Round flower heads. Wet grassy places. 15-30 cm tall. June-Oct.

Fritillary or Snake's Head ▶

Drooping flowers are checkered with light and dark purple. Varies from white to dark purple. Damp meadows. 10 cm tall. May.

You may see these flowers on old walls.

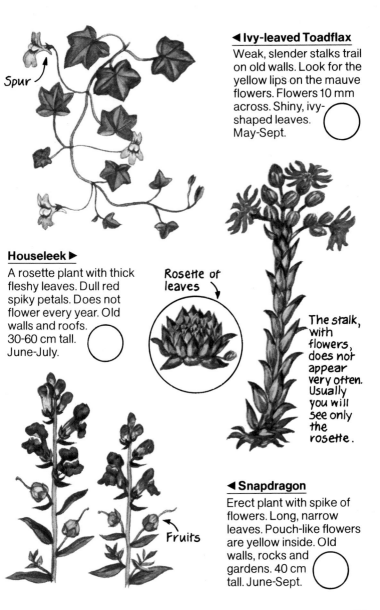

◄ Ivy-leaved Toadflax
Weak, slender stalks trail on old walls. Look for the yellow lips on the mauve flowers. Flowers 10 mm across. Shiny, ivy-shaped leaves. May-Sept.

Spur

Houseleek ►
A rosette plant with thick fleshy leaves. Dull red spiky petals. Does not flower every year. Old walls and roofs. 30-60 cm tall. June-July.

Rosette of leaves

The stalk, with flowers, does not appear very often. Usually you will see only the rosette.

Fruits

◄ Snapdragon
Erect plant with spike of flowers. Long, narrow leaves. Pouch-like flowers are yellow inside. Old walls, rocks and gardens. 40 cm tall. June-Sept.

Look for these flowers on cultivated land.

Scarlet Pimpernel ▶
Grows along the ground.
Flowers close in bad
weather. Black dots under
the pointed oval leaves.
Cultivated land.
15 cm tall.
June-Aug.

Flowers may
also be blue

◀ Poppy
Erect plant with stiff hairs
on stem. Soft red flowers
have dark centres. Round
seed pod. Cornfields and
waste ground. Up
to 60 cm tall.
June-Aug.

Seed pod

Flower
bud

Seed
pod

Long-headed Poppy ▶
Like Poppy, but flowers
are paler and do not have
dark centres. Pod is long
and narrow. Cornfields
and waste ground.
Up to 45 cm tall.
June-Aug.

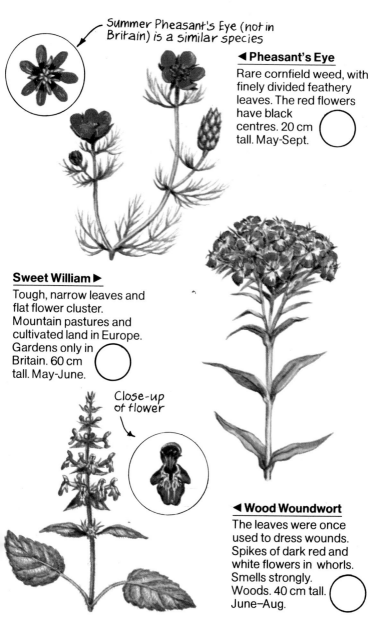

Summer Pheasant's Eye (not in Britain) is a similar species

◀ Pheasant's Eye

Rare cornfield weed, with finely divided feathery leaves. The red flowers have black centres. 20 cm tall. May-Sept.

Sweet William ▶

Tough, narrow leaves and flat flower cluster. Mountain pastures and cultivated land in Europe. Gardens only in Britain. 60 cm tall. May-June.

Close-up of flower

◀ Wood Woundwort

The leaves were once used to dress wounds. Spikes of dark red and white flowers in whorls. Smells strongly. Woods. 40 cm tall. June–Aug.

The flowers on these two pages can be found in woodlands, quite early in the year.

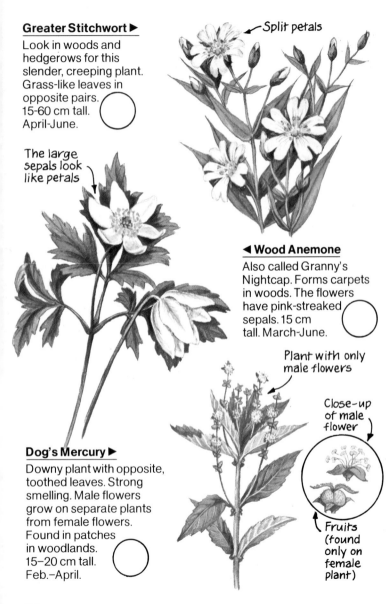

Greater Stitchwort ▶

Look in woods and hedgerows for this slender, creeping plant. Grass-like leaves in opposite pairs. 15-60 cm tall. April-June.

Split petals

The large sepals look like petals

◀ Wood Anemone

Also called Granny's Nightcap. Forms carpets in woods. The flowers have pink-streaked sepals. 15 cm tall. March-June.

Plant with only male flowers

Close-up of male flower

Dog's Mercury ▶

Downy plant with opposite, toothed leaves. Strong smelling. Male flowers grow on separate plants from female flowers. Found in patches in woodlands. 15–20 cm tall. Feb.–April.

Fruits (found only on female plant)

◀ Ramsons or Wood Garlic

Smells of garlic. Broad, bright green leaves grow from a bulb. Forms carpets in damp woods, often with Bluebells.
10-25 cm tall.
April-June.

Notice the long veins that run from one end of the leaf to the other

Lily-of-the-Valley ▶

Grows in dry woods. Broad, dark green leaves and sweet-smelling flowers. Red berries in summer. Also a garden plant. 20 cm tall. May-June.

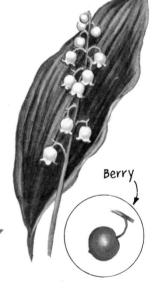

Berry

◀ Snowdrop

Welcomed as the first flower of the new year. Dark green, narrow leaves. Nodding white flowers. Woods.
20 cm tall.
Jan.-March.

Look for these flowers in hedges or woods.

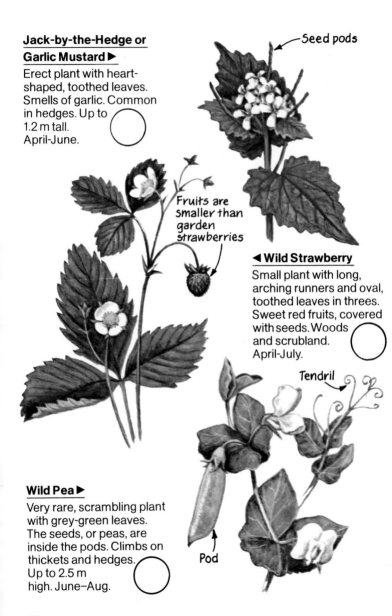

Jack-by-the-Hedge or Garlic Mustard ▶

Erect plant with heart-shaped, toothed leaves. Smells of garlic. Common in hedges. Up to 1.2 m tall. April-June.

Seed pods

Fruits are smaller than garden strawberries

◀ Wild Strawberry

Small plant with long, arching runners and oval, toothed leaves in threes. Sweet red fruits, covered with seeds. Woods and scrubland. April-July.

Tendril

Wild Pea ▶

Very rare, scrambling plant with grey-green leaves. The seeds, or peas, are inside the pods. Climbs on thickets and hedges. Up to 2.5 m high. June–Aug.

Pod

Look for these flowers in hedges and waysides.

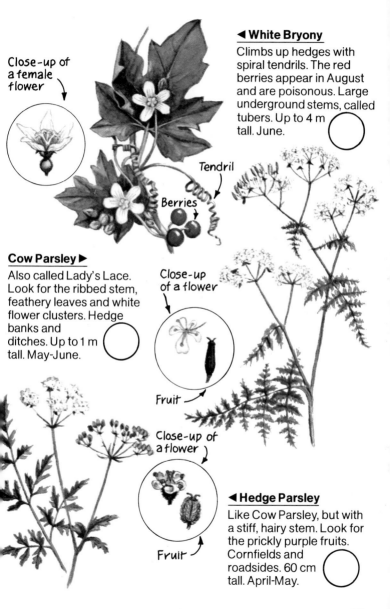

Close-up of a female flower

◀ White Bryony

Climbs up hedges with spiral tendrils. The red berries appear in August and are poisonous. Large underground stems, called tubers. Up to 4 m tall. June.

Tendril

Berries

Cow Parsley ▶

Also called Lady's Lace. Look for the ribbed stem, feathery leaves and white flower clusters. Hedge banks and ditches. Up to 1 m tall. May-June.

Close-up of a flower

Fruit

Close-up of a flower

Fruit

◀ Hedge Parsley

Like Cow Parsley, but with a stiff, hairy stem. Look for the prickly purple fruits. Cornfields and roadsides. 60 cm tall. April-May.

These flowers can be found in or near fresh water (streams, ponds, etc.).

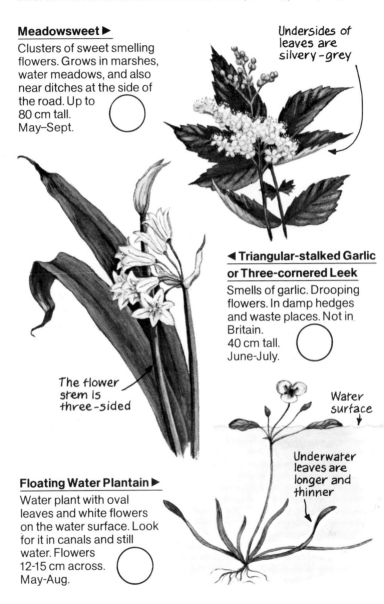

Meadowsweet ▶

Clusters of sweet smelling flowers. Grows in marshes, water meadows, and also near ditches at the side of the road. Up to 80 cm tall. May–Sept.

Undersides of leaves are silvery-grey

The flower stem is three-sided

◀ Triangular-stalked Garlic or Three-cornered Leek

Smells of garlic. Drooping flowers. In damp hedges and waste places. Not in Britain. 40 cm tall. June-July.

Water surface

Underwater leaves are longer and thinner

Floating Water Plantain ▶

Water plant with oval leaves and white flowers on the water surface. Look for it in canals and still water. Flowers 12-15 cm across. May-Aug.

These flowers can be found in or near fresh water (streams, ponds, etc.).

◀ Water Crowfoot
Water plant whose roots are anchored in the mud at the bottom of ponds and streams. Flowers (10–20 mm across) cover the water surface. May–June.

Fine, underwater leaves

These leaves are on the water surface

Water Soldier ▶
Under water except when it flowers. Long saw-like leaves then show above the surface. Flowers 30-40 mm across. Ponds, canals, ditches. June-Aug.

Bud

Runner

◀ Frogbit
Rises to the surface in spring, and spreads with long runners. Shiny round leaves grow in tufts. Flowers 20 mm across. Canals and ponds. July-Aug.

Look for these flowers in fields and other grassy places.

Wild Carrot ▶

Dense clusters of white flowers with a purple flower in the centre. Erect, hairy stem with feathery leaves. Grassy places, often near coast.
60 cm tall.
July–Aug.

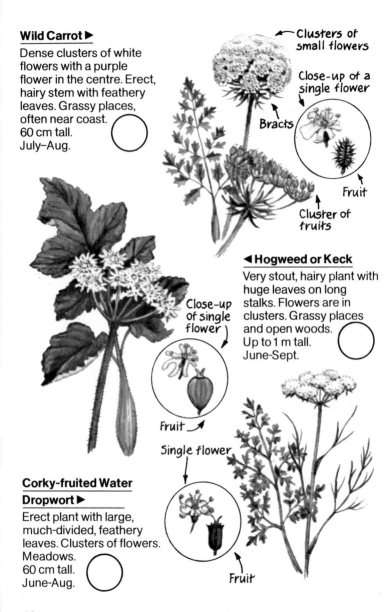

Clusters of small flowers

Close-up of a single flower

Bracts

Fruit

Cluster of fruits

Close-up of single flower

Fruit

◀ Hogweed or Keck

Very stout, hairy plant with huge leaves on long stalks. Flowers are in clusters. Grassy places and open woods.
Up to 1 m tall.
June-Sept.

Single flower

Fruit

Corky-fruited Water Dropwort ▶

Erect plant with large, much-divided, feathery leaves. Clusters of flowers. Meadows.
60 cm tall.
June-Aug.

Look for these flowers in fields and other grassy places.

White petals are sometimes tinged with pink

◄ Daisy
Small plant with rosette of leaves at base. Flowers close at night and in bad weather. Very common on garden lawns.
10 cm tall.
Jan.-Oct.

White or Dutch Clover ►
Creeping plant often grown for animal feed. Look for the white band on the three-lobed leaves. Attracts bees.
10-25 cm tall.
April-Aug.

White band

Runner

Look for the divided petals

◄ Field Mouse-ear Chickweed
Creeping plant with erect stems. Narrow, downy leaves. Grassy places.
10 cm tall.
April-Aug.

Look for these flowers on cultivated land, waste land and waysides.

Nettle ▶

The toothed leaves are covered with stinging hairs. Dangling green-brown flowers. Used to make beer and tea. Common. Up to 1 m tall. June-Aug.

Cluster of flowers

Single flower

Fruit

Close-up of flower

◀ Pigweed or Common Amaranth

Erect hairy plant with large oval leaves. Large spikes of green tufty flowers. Look for it on cultivated land. 50 cm tall. July-Sept.

Close-up of flower

Common Orache ▶

An erect weed with a stiff stem and toothed leaves, both dusty grey. Cultivated land or waste places. Up to 90 cm tall. Aug.-Sept.

Look for these flowers on cultivated land, waste land and waysides.

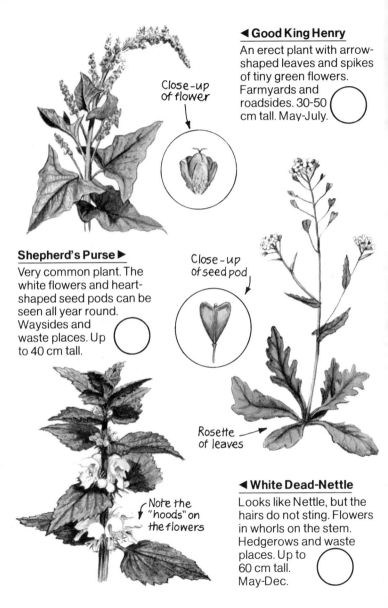

◄ Good King Henry

An erect plant with arrow-shaped leaves and spikes of tiny green flowers. Farmyards and roadsides. 30-50 cm tall. May-July.

Close-up of flower

Shepherd's Purse ►

Very common plant. The white flowers and heart-shaped seed pods can be seen all year round. Waysides and waste places. Up to 40 cm tall.

Close-up of seed pod

Rosette of leaves

Note the "hoods" on the flowers

◄ White Dead-Nettle

Looks like Nettle, but the hairs do not sting. Flowers in whorls on the stem. Hedgerows and waste places. Up to 60 cm tall. May-Dec.

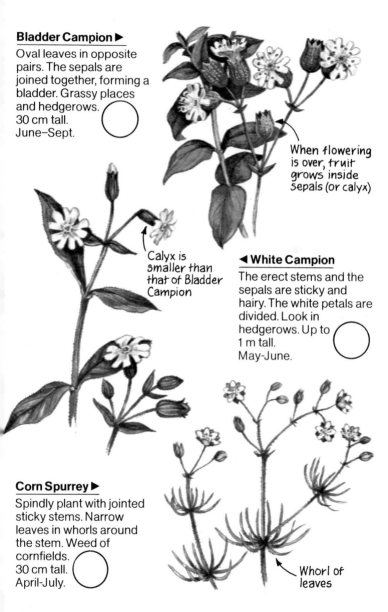

Bladder Campion ▶

Oval leaves in opposite pairs. The sepals are joined together, forming a bladder. Grassy places and hedgerows. 30 cm tall. June–Sept.

When flowering is over, fruit grows inside sepals (or calyx)

Calyx is smaller than that of Bladder Campion

◀ White Campion

The erect stems and the sepals are sticky and hairy. The white petals are divided. Look in hedgerows. Up to 1 m tall. May-June.

Corn Spurrey ▶

Spindly plant with jointed sticky stems. Narrow leaves in whorls around the stem. Weed of cornfields. 30 cm tall. April-July.

Whorl of leaves

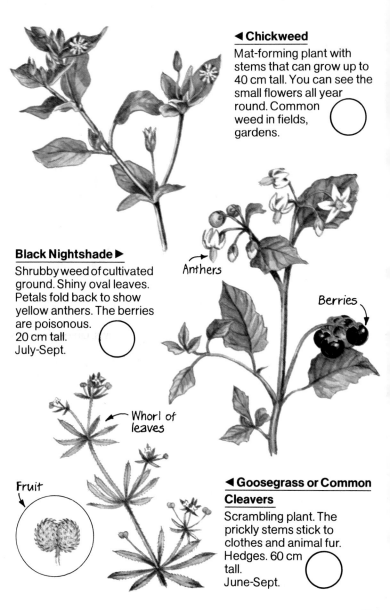

◄ Chickweed

Mat-forming plant with stems that can grow up to 40 cm tall. You can see the small flowers all year round. Common weed in fields, gardens.

Black Nightshade ►

Shrubby weed of cultivated ground. Shiny oval leaves. Petals fold back to show yellow anthers. The berries are poisonous.
20 cm tall.
July-Sept.

Anthers

Berries

Whorl of leaves

Fruit

◄ Goosegrass or Common Cleavers

Scrambling plant. The prickly stems stick to clothes and animal fur. Hedges. 60 cm tall.
June-Sept.

Look for these flowers in grassy places, on waste or cultivated ground.

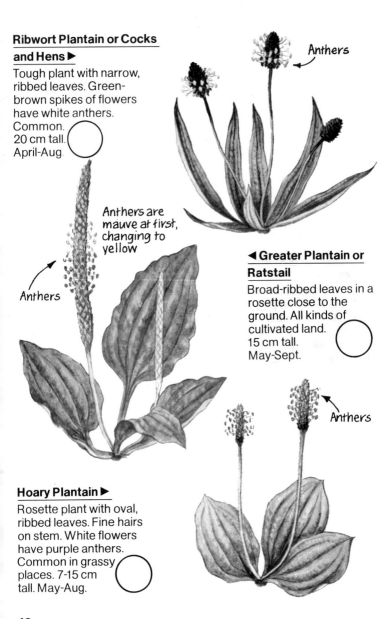

Ribwort Plantain or Cocks and Hens ▶

Tough plant with narrow, ribbed leaves. Green-brown spikes of flowers have white anthers. Common. 20 cm tall. April-Aug.

Anthers

Anthers are mauve at first, changing to yellow

Anthers

◀ Greater Plantain or Ratstail

Broad-ribbed leaves in a rosette close to the ground. All kinds of cultivated land. 15 cm tall. May-Sept.

Anthers

Hoary Plantain ▶

Rosette plant with oval, ribbed leaves. Fine hairs on stem. White flowers have purple anthers. Common in grassy places. 7-15 cm tall. May-Aug.

Look for these flowers on grassy or waste ground.

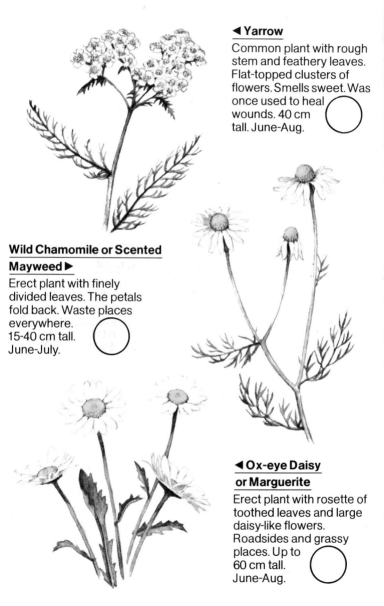

◄ Yarrow
Common plant with rough stem and feathery leaves. Flat-topped clusters of flowers. Smells sweet. Was once used to heal wounds. 40 cm tall. June-Aug.

Wild Chamomile or Scented Mayweed ►
Erect plant with finely divided leaves. The petals fold back. Waste places everywhere. 15-40 cm tall. June-July.

◄ Ox-eye Daisy or Marguerite
Erect plant with rosette of toothed leaves and large daisy-like flowers. Roadsides and grassy places. Up to 60 cm tall. June-Aug.

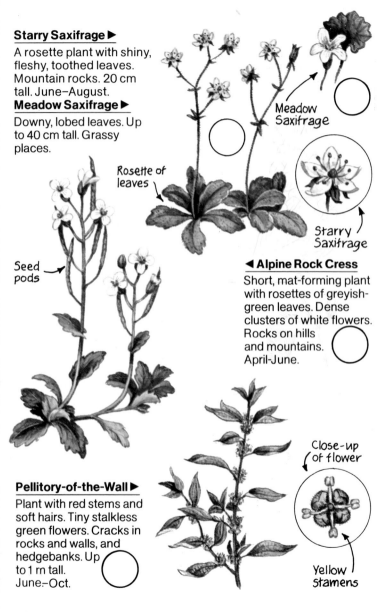

Starry Saxifrage ▶
A rosette plant with shiny, fleshy, toothed leaves. Mountain rocks. 20 cm tall. June–August.

Meadow Saxifrage ▶
Downy, lobed leaves. Up to 40 cm tall. Grassy places.

Meadow Saxifrage

Rosette of leaves

Starry Saxifrage

Seed pods

◀ Alpine Rock Cress
Short, mat-forming plant with rosettes of greyish-green leaves. Dense clusters of white flowers. Rocks on hills and mountains. April-June.

Close-up of flower

Pellitory-of-the-Wall ▶
Plant with red stems and soft hairs. Tiny stalkless green flowers. Cracks in rocks and walls, and hedgebanks. Up to 1 m tall. June.–Oct.

Yellow stamens

Trick Picture Puzzle

These trick pictures show only parts of some of the plants that appear in this book. Can you guess what they are? The answers are upside-down at the bottom of the page.

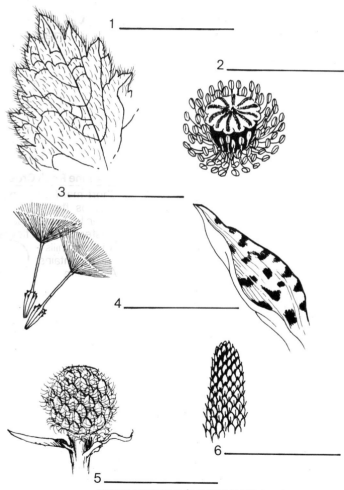

1 _____

2 _____

3 _____

4 _____

5 _____

6 _____

1. Nettle leaf 2. Stigma and stamens of Poppy 3. Dandelion fruits 4. Leaf of Early Purple Orchid 5. Knapweed bud 6. Flower tip of Greater Plantain.

Colouring Quiz

These pictures show outlines of some of the flowers that appear in the book. Can you name them from their shapes and colour them correctly? Their names are upside-down at the bottom of the opposite page.

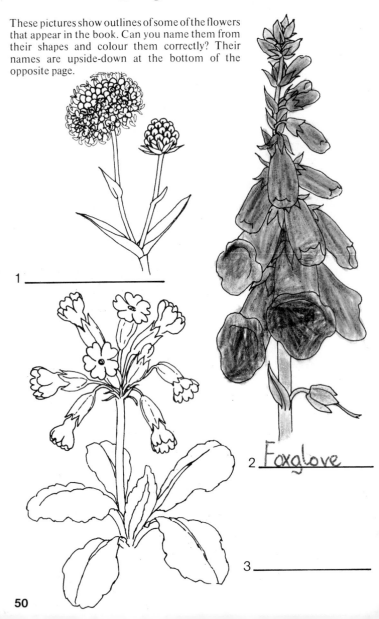

1 _____

2 Foxglove _____

3 _____

4 _____

5 _____

6 _____

7 _Cornflower_

Find the Fruits

The pictures in the middle of these pages show fruits from the same plants as the flowers on these pages. Can you match each fruit with its correct flower? The answers are upside-down at the bottom of the opposite page.

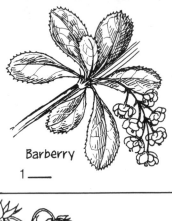

Barberry

1 ___

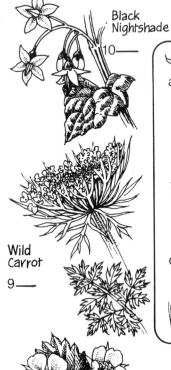

Black Nightshade

10 ___

Wild Carrot

9 ___

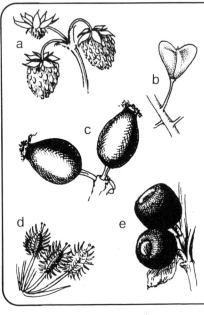

a

b

c

d

e

Wild Strawberry

8 ___

Bilberry

7 ___

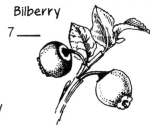

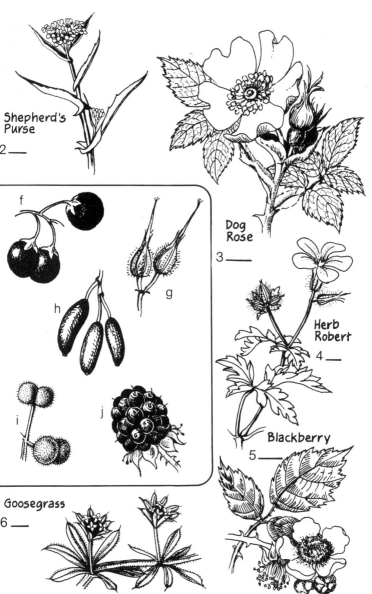

Shepherd's Purse

2 ___

f

g

h

i

j

Dog Rose

3 ___

Herb Robert

4 ___

Blackberry

5 ___

Goosegrass

6 ___

Where do they Grow?

The pictures in the middle of these pages show four places where wild flowers grow. Can you write the correct letter beside each flower's name to show where each one lives? The answers are upside-down at the bottom of the opposite page.

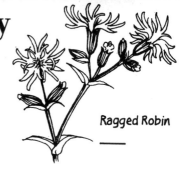

Ragged Robin
__

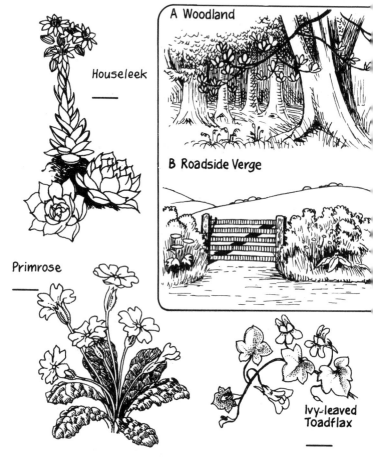

Houseleek
__

A Woodland

B Roadside Verge

Primrose
__

Ivy-leaved Toadflax
__

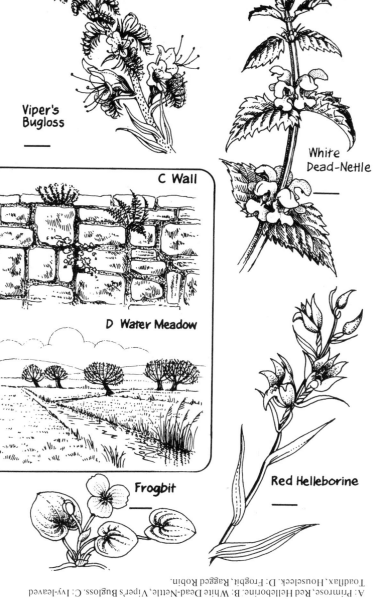

Viper's Bugloss
___

White Dead-Nettle
___

C Wall

D Water Meadow

Frogbit
___

Red Helleborine
___

Make a Flower Notebook

Choose a spot near your home to study plants that grow there. If you live in the country, find a wide, grassy roadside verge or a disused railway cutting for your study.

If you are in a town, choose an empty garden, a churchyard or a grassy bank beside a canal. These are all areas where plants have had a long time to grow undisturbed, so you will be able to find many different kinds.

Mark out about a square metre of ground with sticks and string. Count and identify the flowers growing there and measure their height. Note how many of the same plants you see.

Try to find out why they grow in the same area. You could choose and mark out another study area where different plants grow and compare the ones you find with those in your other area.

Look carefully at the picture below. It shows a study area marked out on a grassy bank. Can you identify the plants growing there? They are Daisy, Nettle, Red Campion, Larkspur, Greater Plantain, Bird's Foot Trefoil and Dandelion.

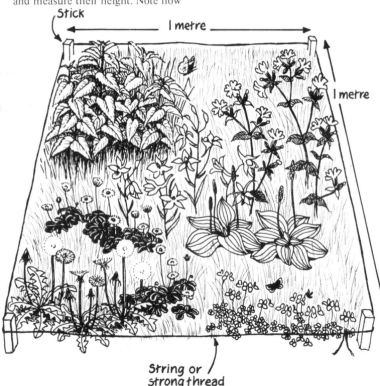

Stick

I metre

I metre

String or strong thread

Make a notebook to record changes in the flowers you find throughout the year. Use a loose-leaf binder or an exercise book. Draw only one plant on a page and write down where you found it.

You can also pick very common flowers and press them, to illustrate your book. Put the flower between two pieces of blotting paper and rest some heavy books on it. When it is dry, carefully stick it into your book with a spot of glue.

On the opposite page, make a chart and note changes in the appearance of the plant in different seasons. If a new plant starts to grow in your study area, make a page for it. Look out, too, for butterflies and other insects. Note which plants they feed on and look for butterfly eggs on the leaves.

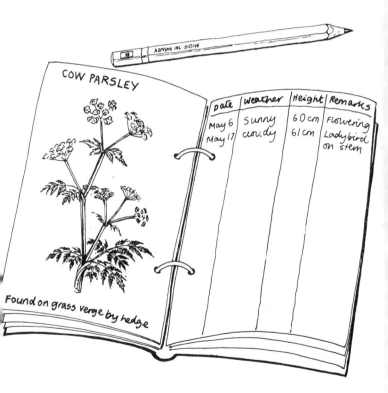

COW PARSLEY

Found on grass verge by hedge

Date	Weather	Height	Remarks
May 6	Sunny	60 cm	Flowering
May 17	cloudy	61 cm	Ladybird on stem

Photographing Flowers

Photographs make a good record of the flowers you spot. Stick your photos into an album, label them, and write notes about where you spotted the flowers, their height, and other details. Cut photographs of flowers out of magazines and add them to your collection.

Here are some tips to help you to take successful photographs.

Use a colour film. Always take photographs with the sun behind you and make sure that your shadow does not fall on the flower. Try to photograph the whole plant so that the stem and leaves are visible.

With a simple camera, you cannot photograph flowers in close-up, so choose your flower carefully. Tiny flowers photographed from a distance will not show up at all. A tall plant with large flowers or a patch of creeping plants will make good photographs.

If you lie flat on the ground and photograph a flower from below,

outlined against the sky, it will stand out clearly. Sunlight filtering through the leaves shows up the veins in them.

To prevent a flower from being lost among grass and leaves, you can prop a piece of black or coloured card behind it and photograph it against this background.

If you want to photograph flowers in a wood, where the light is dim, experiment with a flash cube.

Be sure to make notes about the flowers when you photograph them. Refer to these notes when you are writing in your photo album.

Sea Pink
Portland
on cliffs
16 May 1977
Height 12cm
also on beach

Wild Arum
Hedge bank in
Marshwood Vale
20 May Height 25 cm

Primrose
Hatch Wood
4 April
Height 12cm

Marsh Mallow
beside River Frome
Aug 27 Height 1m

Corn Marigold
edge of barley field
Loders Farm, Cerne
24 June Height 30cm

Books to Read

The Wild Flowers of Britain and Northern Europe. R. Fitter, A. Fitter, M. Blamey (Collins). Easy to use, light to carry, cheap reference paperback.
The Concise British Flora in Colour. W. Keble Martin (Ebury Press/Michael Joseph). Large book, good illustrations.
The Concise Flowers of Europe. O. Polunin (Oxford University Press). Photos and short descriptions.
The Nature Trail Book of Wild Flowers. S. Tarsky (Usborne). Cheap. How to study and record flowers. Lots of interesting ideas.

Wild Flowers of the Spring. G. E. Hyde (Warne).
Wild Flowers of the Summer. G. E. Hyde (Warne). Small, cheap, reference books with photographs.
Wild Flowers. John Hutchinson (Penguin).
Wild Flowers of Europe. Lorna F. Bowden (Hamlyn).
Mountain Flowers. A. Huxley (Blandford).
Wild Flowers of Britain. Roger Phillips (Pan). Very good photographs.

Clubs to Join

The Council For Nature (address: The Zoological Gardens, Regent's Park. London NW1 4RY) is a representative body of more than 450 societies, and will supply the addresses of your local *Natural History Societies*. (Send a stamped, addressed envelope for their free list). Many of these have wild flower sections and almost all have field meetings. The Council will also give you the address of your local *County Naturalist Trust,* which may have a junior branch. Many of the Trusts have meetings, lectures, and opportunities for work on nature reserves.
London Natural History Society The Secretary, 21 Green Way, Frinton on Sea, Essex, and the *Botanical Society of the British Isles,* c/o The Natural History Museum, Cromwell Road, London SW7. Both societies encourage young members, but their journals are quite advanced and it would be best to join when you really know your wild flowers.
The British Naturalist Association (Mrs K. L. Butcher, Willowfield, Boynes Wood Road, Four Marks, Alton, Hants) would be more suitable to join, and the *Wild Life Youth Service* (Wallington, Surrey) is a special society just for young people, with projects and a quarterly newsletter.
One of the best societies to join is *The Wild Flower Society* (address: c/o Harvest House, 62 London Road, Reading). They help you with identification, organize competitions, and when you join, give you a collecting diary where you can record every wild flower that you spot.

Index

Scorecard

The flowers in this scorecard are arranged in the same order as they appear in the book. When you go spotting, fill in the date at the top of one of the blank columns, and then write in that column your score, next to each flower that you see. At the end of the day, add up your scores and put the total at the bottom of the columns. Then add up your grand total.

Page	Species (Name of flower)	Score	Date	Date	Date	Page	Species (Name of flower)	Score			
8	Lesser Celandine	5				14	Golden Rod	10			
8	Alternate-leaved Golden Saxifrage	15				15	Rape	5			
8	Creeping Buttercup	5				15	Cypress Spurge	15			
9	Creeping Jenny	15				15	Wild Pansy	10			
9	Cowslip	10				16	Cornflower	25			
9	Common Meadow Rue	15				16	Larkspur	15			
10	Wood Avens	10				16	Lesser Periwinkle	15			
10	Yellow Pimpernel	10				17	Viper's Bugloss	10			
10	Barberry	15				17	Common Forget-me-not	10			
11	Wood Groundsel	15				17	Common Speedwell	10			
11	Yellow Archangel	10				18	Monkshood	20			
11	Primrose	10				18	Brooklime	10			
12	Gorse/Furze	10				18	Bugle	10			
12	Bird's Foot Trefoil	10				19	Sea Holly	15			
12	Creeping Cinquefoil	5				19	Meadow Clary	20			
12	Silverweed	10				19	Bluebell	10			
13	Common St John's Wort	10				20	Wood Sorrel	5			
13	Woad	20				20	Blackberry	5			
13	Dandelion	5				20	Dog Rose	15			
14	Stonecrop	10				21	Bistort	10			
14	Purslane	15				21	Gt Bindweed	10			
	Total						Total				

Page	Species (Name of flower)	Score				Page	Species (Name of flower)	Score			
21	Red Helleborine	25				29	Tufted Vetch	10			
22	Knotgrass	5				29	Common Dog Violet	10			
22	Soapwort	20				30	Pasque Flower	25			
22	Common Fumitory	10				30	Field Scabious	10			
23	Sand Spurrey	10				30	Devil's Bit Scabious	10			
23	Rosebay Willowherb	5				30	Fritillary	20			
23	Herb Robert	10				31	Ivy-leaved Toadflax	5			
24	Ling/Heather	5				31	Houseleek	15			
24	Bell Heather	15				31	Snapdragon	5			
24	Bilberry	10				32	Scarlet Pimpernel	10			
25	Sorrel	5				32	Poppy	10			
25	Sheep's Sorrel	15				32	Long-headed Poppy	5			
25	Common Centaury	10				33	Pheasant's Eye	25			
26	Ragged Robin	15				33	Summer Pheasant's Eye	25			
26	Knapweed	10				33	Sweet William	20			
26	Hemp Agrimony	10				33	Wood Woundwort	10			
27	Deptford Pink	25				34	Greater Stitchwort	5			
27	Blood-red Geranium	10				34	Wood Anemone	10			
27	Red Campion	10				34	Dog's Mercury	10			
28	Early Purple Orchid	15				35	Ramsons	15			
28	Foxglove	10				35	Lily-of the Valley	15			
28	Policeman's Helmet	15				35	Snowdrop	15			
28	Touch-me-not Balsam	25				36	Garlic Mustard	5			
29	Bats in the Belfry	15				36	Wild Strawberry	15			
	Total						Total				

Page	Species (Name of flower)	Score			
36	Wild Pea	20			
37	White Bryony	15			
37	Cow Parsley	5			
37	Hedge Parsley	15			
38	Meadowsweet	10			
38	Triangular-stalked Garlic	20			
38	Floating Water Plantain	15			
39	Water Crowfoot	10			
39	Water Soldier	25			
39	Frogbit	15			
40	Wild Carrot	10			
40	Hogweed/Keck	5			
40	Corky-fruited Water Dropwort	25			
41	Daisy	5			
41	White Clover	5			
41	Field Mouse-ear Chickweed	15			
42	Nettle	5			
42	Pigweed	10			
42	Common Orache	5			
43	Good King Henry	5			
43	Shepherd's Purse	5			
43	Wt Dead-Nettle	5			

Page	Species (Name of flower)	Score			
44	Bladder Campion	10			
44	White Campion	10			
44	Corn Spurrey	10			
45	Chickweed	5			
45	Black Nightshade	10			
45	Goosegrass	5			
46	Ribwort Plantain	5			
46	Greater Plantain	5			
46	Hoary Plantain	5			
47	Yarrow	5			
47	Wild Chamomile	15			
47	Ox-eye Daisy	10			
48	Starry Saxifrage	15			
48	Meadow Saxifrage	20			
48	Alpine Rock Cress	20			
48	Pellitory-of-the-Wall	15			

Total

Total

Grand Total